Nap Time

with Imani and the Fox

Fulton Books
Meadville, PA

Published by Fulton Books 2023

ISBN 979-8-88505-336-5 (paperback)
ISBN 979-8-88505-337-2 (digital)
ISBN 979-8-88982-225-7 (hardcover)

Printed in the United States of America

It's nap time now, and I can't sleep. What do I do instead?
I wiggle my toes, play with my feet,
and count the braids on my head.

1

Nap Time

with Imani and the Fox

Lena Bee

It's nap time now, and I can't sleep. What do I do instead?
I think about cows and count some sheep
on a farm or old homestead.

4

It's nap time now, and I can't sleep. What do I do instead?
I shiver like snowmen who play in sleet
and ride on a slippery sled.

5

It's nap time now, and I can't sleep. What do I do instead?
I'll blow bubbles like sharks in the ocean deep,
and a surfboard is my bed.

It's nap time now, and I can't sleep. What do I do instead?
I listen for cars that toot and beep
and stop at lights that are red.

It's nap time now, and I can't sleep. What do I do instead?
I feel the blast of a rocket fleet...
so far into space, they sped.

It's nap time now, and I can't sleep. What do I do instead?
I pretend to travel to a swamp with fleas
and meet a nice frog named Ned.

It's naptime now, and I can't sleep. What do I do instead?

I feel feathers, umbrellas, drums, and beads.

It's a Mardi Gras parade I lead.

It's nap time now, and I can't sleep. What do I do instead?
I remember all the times the fox hugs me
because I walk her and make sure she's fed.

19

It's nap time now, and I can't sleep. What do I do instead?
I watch my friends who slumber and sleep.

Dedicated to:

Imani E. Stanley

Love,

Lena 🐑

&

Jasmina Cazacu

Love,

Jesse 🖌

Lesson Plan

Phonics

- Children will be able to differentiate short *e* and long *e* vowel sounds.
- Children will be able to differentiate vowel combinations that make the short *e* sound in words.
- Children will be able to differentiate vowel combinations that make the long *e* sound in words.
- Children will be able to identify at least twenty level 1 sight words.

Social-Emotional Development

- Children will practice ways to self soothe and calm themselves without the help of another.
- Children will practice the skill of occupying oneself while waiting.
- Children will master the skill of respecting others' needs and wants.
- Caregivers can observe a continuity of positive emotional processing as a result of resting.

Health, Safety, and Nutrition

- Caregivers can help children discern the importance of rest and napping.
- Caregivers can help children understand that rest time allows for one's mind and body to recharge.
- Caregivers can use visual cues from the illustrations to ensure that the mood, time, and length is appropriate for nap time.

Cognitive

- Children will practice pattern recognition.
- Children will enhance hiding and finding objects to increase object-permanence skills.
- Children will assimilate and accommodate routines and procedures.

A Little about This Book

Imani and the fox are an inseparable duo. They are both three years old. The fox is Imani's pet who is not able to go to school with Imani, so Imani has a stuffed fox that looks exactly like her to take to school. This story takes place in Imani's preschool classroom, where she normally has a challenging time winding down for rest time. The children rest on preschool cots, and children are allowed a warm blanket and a lovey (soft toy) to rest with. Unfortunately, Imani cannot sleep; however, Imani is wise enough to practice imagery to occupy herself while the other children engage in nap time.

About the Author

 Lanesa Bejnarowicz is also known as Lena Bee because she loves children and animals. She received a master's in education while she lived in Honolulu, Hawaii. She also lived in Chicago, Illinois; Philadelphia, Pennsylvania; Duluth, Minnesota; and Clarksville, Tennessee. Lena is a former reading specialist, kindergarten teacher, and preschool administrator. Lena is a self-proclaimed arborist who loves to spend time with her husband, grandchildren, and two dogs on their fifty-acre tree farm. She especially loves writing books for children.

Printed in the USA
CPSIA information can be obtained
at www.ICGtesting.com
JSHW040300050823
45036JS00011B/19